PHASES

THE JOURNEY OF LIFE THROUGH POETRY

PARTHIV RHYTHM DAS

Copyright © Parthiv Rhythm Das
All Rights Reserved.

This book has been published with all efforts taken to make the material error-free after the consent of the author. However, the author and the publisher do not assume and hereby disclaim any liability to any party for any loss, damage, or disruption caused by errors or omissions, whether such errors or omissions result from negligence, accident, or any other cause.

While every effort has been made to avoid any mistake or omission, this publication is being sold on the condition and understanding that neither the author nor the publishers or printers would be liable in any manner to any person by reason of any mistake or omission in this publication or for any action taken or omitted to be taken or advice rendered or accepted on the basis of this work. For any defect in printing or binding the publishers will be liable only to replace the defective copy by another copy of this work then available.

To my mother, Anindita Ghosh

Who raised and nurtured me with her strength.

To my beloved teacher, Papiya Ghosh

Who has been the epitome of inspiration while jotting down my ideas.

Contents

Contents

Foreword

By Papiya Ghosh

'Phases- The journey of life through poetry' is a prepossessing book comprising of some of the most simple yet subtle, deep and meaningful poems. The series of poetry represents the creative imagination of the poet's mind.

The poetries express extraordinary emotions. It feels extremely wonderful to be a part of this book written by my best and sincere student Parthiv Rhythm Das. Being his guide is really delightful, as we built a literary alliance more than teaching and learning.

Through this book Parthiv has manifested the stages of human life using his poetic skills. Starting with poems like **"A father's promise"**, **"Raspberry"**, **"Playthings"** the book hits the road of poems like **"Bleed with Pride"**, **"Falling Down"**, **"An appeal to Death"** while ending with a bonus surprise. From innocence to experience the book has touched every topic delicately with fine interpretation. Parthiv has given equal importance to burning issues like climate change and women's safety through his poetry, which is really worth mentioning.

Without revealing much about the book I would urge everyone to read the book for once, to get into the depth of the poems. Each poetry has its own aura and depict a story that people of any age can connect with. It will let you travel to the olden days of childhood, bringing nostalgia and memories. The book eventually celebrate aging with the significance of Nature in one's life. This was indeed a congenial read.

Acknowledgements

I pay my highest obeisance and gratitude to His Divine Lotus feet, Lord Krishna, whose blessing is an eternal foundation of how I live my life.

Bringing into knowledge, I offer my infinite thanks to all those friends, literary experts, mentors and common men whose synergies in radiance or darkness inspired me come up with my debut book **'PHASES- The journey of Life through Poetry'.** I'm grateful to the publishing platform, Notion Press for providing me the golden opportunity to publish my poetry collection under their easy and subtle course of action.

I would like to thank my mother, **Anindita Ghosh** for supporting my decision to work on this book efficiently. I am forever grateful to her for the love she showered upon me and the courage she gave for this endeavour.

Limitless thanks to my own childhood teacher **Papiya Ghosh**, a fine literary scholar and an intellectual person who served as the living inspiration of my life, teaching me not only the English literature but also imbibed an immense interest in the subject. My utmost gratification to her!

My deepest gratitude to **Ankur Hazarika**, a very close friend of mine, for providing much assistance and support right from generalizing the conception and deciding the title of the book. I cannot thank him enough for making my work easy and pointing out the errors at an earliest. Without him the book would not have been materialized.

My heartfelt thanks to **Shibangi Saha**, my forever best friend, for guiding and assisting me with various strategies and ideas to launch the book. She has been the guiding light of this journey who not only spent her valuable time giving suggestions to me; but strengthened my enthusiasm with her inspiring words.

I also extend my thanks to **Kaushika Sarma**, my forever bosom mate for adding more to my passion of writing, encouraging me and hearing me out at times of distress. No work can be completed without motivation. So my special thanks to **Devitrishna Thakuria**, best friend cum sister and **Anwesha Saha** an online mate, sharing a very spectacular poetic bond with me. I thank them for constantly motivating me to write the book and appreciate my work through their compliments.

Countless thanks to everyone who have crossed their paths and helped me to shape this book and bring into publish my first ever book of Poetry Collection. Last but not the least I offer my sincere thanks to you- all my dearest readers for picking up this book.

Without the generous love, blessings and support of my parents, family, mates, and well wishers, my attempt to write this book would be incomplete. Without your accompaniment the journey of this writer would not have been that easy. I hope that my words will create wonders in your life and bring out the various facets of life.

Preface

Have you ever sat there with your diary and not known what to write? It is a situation of uncertainty but then picking up the poetry book, reading through different excerpts can help you blossom the suppressed perceptions in mind; you never knew existed. Poetry is an incredible language of love that uses a composition of words to express the highest order of imagination, an unremitting method of fabricating the feelings of real and imaginary world. Poetry is benevolent for the soul, whether in relation to normal beings or poet themselves. Turning into the symphony of poetry, poetry is a rhythmical journey in the splendid path of isolation. It's the brevity of expressions with a magic of poetic devices, simplifying a prolonged story in a few lines of complexity.

For me writing poetry is comparative to painting in the canvas, fusing it with meaning, emotions, words, sounds and rhythm that the eternal eyes can view. From a young age we are taught to recite and read poetry of renounced poets in high schools. And as the time goes by, we discover a strange interest in writing but lack the confidence to touch the pen. At that point take we must pick up the pen and jot down whatever comes in the mind. Hence I often say, **"Everyone is a writer of his own imagination. While some write in pages others just recite monologue in the mind."** Poetry is so important that it help us to manifest and appreciate the world around us. It is a bridge, an instantaneous path to change the outlook for a broader picture. Poetry is about constructing a world less about tearing each other down and apart, and more about coming together, helping us to realize that we're not as different as we think. And despite our differences, we feel the same grief, pain, joy or happiness. Reading and writing poetry is of greater good, whose benefits are rebuilding a more connected and caring world.

When I was navigating through the internal aspects of life I felt the sensation to share my poetical works relating it with life, Nature, emotions, love, darkness and reality checks. I tried to create a small world of poetry, compiling a list of collected poems that I wrote to satisfy the breadth and width of most poetic souls. **PHASES-THE JOURNEY OF LIFE THROUGH POETRY** is a journey of poems right from the traditional aspect to the avant-garde poems, describing each phase of Life.

I invite you- you the young, budding and newbie writers just like me and all my dear readers- to open these pages and discover a new flavor of poetry in each page. I invite you to explore the world of my poetry, to relearn the magic of poetry.

Let's get there, together.

Author's Note

I never had a dream of publishing or writing poetry, much less to be described as a poet. I discovered poetry only when I took my pen and started jotting down my ideas. And in no time there was spontaneous overflow of powerful emotions to create my first poem at the age of fourteen. But I stepped away from the virtue of writing to chase down my studies but managed to write short poems in my diary. Trust me now! these short poems are magical entity that highlights a deep analysis of a perfect moral. I've also learnt during this time, not to throw the short poems because these lines might serve to create a massive poetry one day in future.

As my first poem *(entitled as 'My Mother')*, got selected for publishing in my school annual magazine, my heart found a new rhythm from the echoes of an old melody that sing the songs of motivation for my writing. It was like I never stepped away from my passion and since then I never stopped writing.

As a newbie, I didn't worry much about style or a perfect format but to learn the basic rule of writing. In that case, I was much helped by English tutor coupled with various articles, poetic patterns, books and symmetries of word in a poem. This is how the craze of reading and writing went on and on. Writing poetry is like painting in canvas with all the imagination that keeps on flowing from one corner of brain to other. We all are predictable to the saying, *"A pictures paints thousands of words and a beautiful story trying to persuade a complex idea which can be more*

effectively demonstrated by a single image, that image being able to convey or portray the meaning more essentially than a description." I actively started writing poetry when lockdown hit India, giving me some time to flourish through my passion. I wrote poems as an outlet of feelings purely for myself and never did I think of publishing one. But with the passing time I became ambitious and in the eagerness to achieve recognition, I put into print my first ever co- authored book entitled as ***Shhh... No one needs to know*** containing one of my poems. As a writer the feeling of excitement began long before publishing the book. Excitement is what gave me the initial impetus to begin with the writing project.

Writing is an integral part of my life that creates my sole hobby. Writing poetry involves both a part of enthusiasm and exhaustion. It is an engrossing matter for me, so it's definitely a dream like journey that requires safe driving and proper reach to the destination with patience. In order to articulate various matters- like the beauty of spring, the beautiful sunset, the captivating evening or a murder mystery, words need to create feelings what others cannot create and that is the power of a poet. Poetry being such a deep creativity is always energetic and tiring. The inconvenience and intolerance in the world also add fuel to the exhaustion. So basically after a long process of hard work comprising of excitement, passion, enthusiasm, exhaustion and imagination, the final product of poetry is somehow a feeling worth sharing.

"*As long as I have been able to write, I desire to be a writer.*
The longing to become a poet doesn't create books alone;

but it encloses the entire society in the pen of the writer's imaginative and real world."

~ Parthiv Rhythm Das

Poetry

A semi-illusionary writing
having no rhymes or
composed with the symphony
of rhythmic words that,
imaginately resonates with
reality and imagination;
a part of subconscious mind and
the metaphysical phenomenon of existence
where ingenuity is layered with
poetic devices and undying realism.

Written for the masses

Tailored for the niche

Childhood- A Garden of Memories

Childhood memories! It's like a garden consisting of prismatic flowers each having a unique essence and a particular aroma, barely coinciding with one another. Writing about childhood and its element is often narrative that includes either the perspective of the child or of an adult reflecting on their childhood memories. Childhood literature can also combine social codes with a pinch of entertainment. I've tried combing all the aspects of childhood writing, may it be from the child's view point or my own experience, alongside raising social concern and codes.

Let's unfurl the poems dedicated only for 'Childhood'.

1. Treasured Offspring

All birds of paradise

warble in blithe,

Bells of heaven

chime in delight and

Earth rejuvenates in spring.

Fluttering zephyr bring

All dulcet tunes together,
Changing the rhythmic course,
Unto far more beautiful melodies,
That the world could ever hear.
Forty winks of golden hue
kiss his eyes,
And smile adulates
the moment he rise.
Dozing under the lap,
Tiny toad tuned to the lullaby,
With dreams more euphonic and
bliss so sweeter.
Behind each star
hides an ecstatic dream,
But to reveal its path
The child needs to sleep.
In the bouncy chair he rests,
A bestowed gift
Dropped in the address of
love and nurture.

2. Save the Daughter's Voice

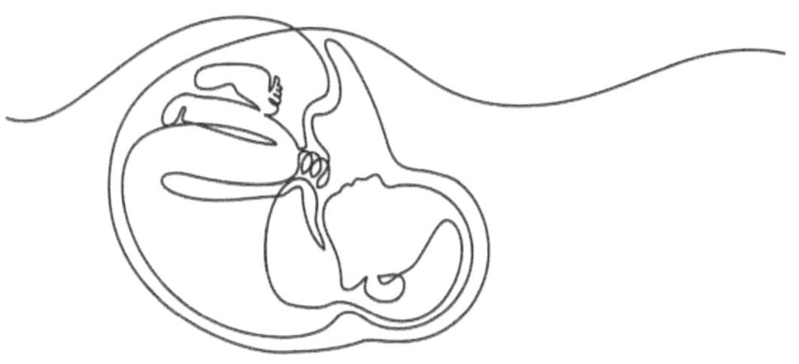

Uniting in the ties of love
Two seperate souls
pledged for eternity.
Gradual elapse of time,
a face unseen intrigued
the core attention there.
Expectancy diffused in the air
with cherry and full of care,

As they wait for a child- a new face
To carry forward the parental race.
Through the layers
of cell and blood,
Wrapped in the mother's womb,
The child jest
in movement joyful.
Rejoicing in delight,
The night embellishes with light.
Gathering glitters of joy indoor,
The whole little world
Yearns for the baby's smile.
Nine-month phase was edging towards
And suddenly a shrill voice
echoed the room,
There she arrived
a sacred duty so beautiful.
In the duvet bed she lied,
Dreaming of her mother
slept so close by.
Everyone joined the flow in happiness,
But to know the voice- the child, a girl
Glow faded as dry as dust
And all dreams went in vain.
Because the girl was a mother's blame.
Waves of protest
raised in societal fear,

To slay a soul
before it could rear.
Hearing this mother stood for mutiny,
To protect her new born progeny.
Mother unleashed
her warth and rage,
To liberate her daughter
from the demonic cage.
Tormenting a tender heart
is never a brave choice,
The prayer says
To save a daughter's voice.
Let her smile glow in the light
Let her live a harmonious life,
Not as a choice
but as an eternal right.

3. Reflections of an Unequivocal Love

The only love better than

Almighty's love

Is the unequivocal love of a mother,

That spread like the Deodar

A shelter, a guardian,

a home forever.

The child was crafted within her,

It is also true that

The child was created for her.

The arms were sculpted

Into cradle,

to hold her child,

And babbles of her baby

Was a melody

soothing her humdrum mind.

Watching securely

in every sight,

Memorizing smiles and

tracing frowns,

She records her tiny moves.

A chorus in the

zephyr she starts,

To calm the sobbing neonate

Behind the tuneful art.

She brings caramel of glee,

Sweets of aloud laughter and

Perches wisdom as vast as a sea.

Despite of thousands flusters,

She discover something

in her child,

To enshrine, to admire and

to love.

4. A father's Promise

When you feel an arm

Rest upon your forehead

And you hear

a low deep thrum,

I hope you dream

gladly of your father.

Along with your arrival

Responsibility visited my house,

For it's a winsome start,
From now and forever more.
I hold you like
gleam in my eyes,
Cherish your aura
in my hidden glimpses
And hope to you
it already shows.
An oath I've sworn
Not just to protect but
to cherish and always love.
From the day you arrived
I have never felt so alive,
Living those perfect moments
of fatherhood.
Bringing bliss
straight to my life
I adore you my child-
A splendid gift of my lifetime.

5. Euphony of Paradise

The world is on pause,

As troubles send-off.

Happiness fabricates the home,

Blazing fireflies allure,

As the child speaks

in moments joyful.

How tempting!

the voice of innocent heart,

That sparkle
our dim souls and
We powered up for millennia,
In the battery of infinite energy.
Behind the silencing of the clock
Voice of the child is a door,
To escape the chaos so bore.
As mother narrates
the story with a plot,
His babbling voice and
clenching fist
Conveys gaiety in a gist.
In a brief moment of bliss,
Soaring our zest with no limits,
We lend an ear to the child,
To hear the euphony of Paradise.

6. A Spiritual Smile

From the endearment
of mother's arms
The infant smiled
in the lighted room.
Singing, perching, and murmuring,
Sparrows and robins

visit round the clock,
To have a view of
her spiritual smile.
Her eyes like prismatic crystal,
Refracts luminescence
of her heart and love abound.
The toddler as it
tuned to her childhood,
The darkened sights that
Chocked the mind once,
Fades away with her beam.
The melancholic silence that
Quietened the eardrums once,
Has been gently soothed
with her ever-growing squeal.
A poet could not be but glee
To see the artistry of
a growing child -
The splash of magic
upon her family
In the unique landscape of her genesis.

7. Down the Memory Lane

The school stand
still by the road,
An indigent man
selling ice creams;
Beside the wall
the shrubberies grow
And Cassia petals

scatter in the floor.
As the eyes look far and wide
The wooden desk and bench,
The fissured floors,
the battered seats,
Reminds of the nine hour class.
The feet that crawl
slow to school,
Went storming out to write.
Once a furious sun dazzled upon
The apple kissed cheeks,
And little eyes full of weeps,
Feared to put forth
his delayed steps.
For hours he stood,
low upon a face
Where pride and shame intermingled.
Shoving with impatient feet,
The sand he lingered and
With restless tiny hands,
Reddish uniform he fingered.
Leisurely the sun sets,
The soft dazzle
caressing the cheeks same,
As if a fault she confessed.
Greetings with
tearful laugh and

Expressing her
abundant love,
The gray-haired lady
blesses for triumph.
Several years have passed,
She spent an age,
Experienced her life,
Still in the room of vacant origin
She yearns.

8. Child- like Happiness

Wide eyes, diffused in wonders
Contemplate the world as fonders:
Visioning the sunrise
for the first time and
Believing the whole nine yards,
We trusted the dinkum oil or
Stories of fiction.
Childhood begins with faith,
A new maxim on fresh eyes -
Deeming mistakes
with pretty estimates,
Playing with truthful lies.
Of prickly circs and
sorrowful apparent,
we gain our skills,
For personage to anticipate.
Basked with
the warm sunlight,
Escorted with
crazy laughters,
We bring the playground jollity,
To an ever more
heartwarming hues.

Twilight adieu us,
scarlet sky arises and
In search of the downy lap
We marched home together.

9. Playthings

A dried up pond,
blooming kashful
A tree of gulmohor and
hanging honeycomb,
Lies behind the vibrant school.
Crowded with children,
Soaked through clay,
Beneath the willows,
Sunrays felt not
so warm that day.
As the surging mynah
Tuned into his
sweet-toned notes,
The children set
aback to perceive,
If people confound it
as a musical track.
The sole banyan tree,
rooted and standstill,
A grassy surface - spare the perfect locus
For hide and seek games.
The games with rhyme and
broken twigs,

Absorbed in mud-pies and
uneven sticks,
Skipping and whirling,
Jumping in the hopscotch,
Then war and fight sometime,
Hollering into
an empty play
Until the game
ends with a chime.

10. Raspberry

The silence of August evening,
Of music in the silver drops
Poured heavy rain and
sun for a week,
For the raspberries

to ripen in the boughs.
Silken silky shine of red clot
Berries in black, purple and
golden also shimmer.
Consuming one from the basket,
raw and sweet,
Like old wine -
saccharine blood was in it.
Leaving stains of craving,
We pluck more from the yard,
As red drupelets piled up the hunger.
Sent us with oil-cans,
flour-tins and jam-pots
We trekked and picked,
Round the hayfields and amid the meadows,
Until the cans were brimming full.
As pepper sprinkles on the top
Our hands turned like a plate,
And mouth slickens
with reddish paint.
Spear-grass prickles the trousers,
Pebbles aching the sole
But the jars we hoarded
were crammed full.
Then the juice was pungent,
The fruit fermented,
sweetness went off;

One off the bush, Grandma was all set
To concoct the raspberry jam.
Eyes dimming with tears
We felt down the dumps
For all the lovely canfuls
that would taste sour now.

11. A Polychromatic Song

Sultry sun on the
green grassland,
Calmly engulfs the day.
The overlapping
clouds in the sky
Rumbles the
advancing storm,
Feathered finches that
breathe in the wind
Quickly fly to their
nest in the trees.
The darkness expands
a blanket of velvety black,
Hugging the earth
as she dreams.
Thunderous culverin
explode the sky
With megawatt light
that pierces the eye.
Icy rain cascading from
a confident sky,
Quenches the soil and
life depending on it.

The darkened sky
start to slow,
And sultry sun
flickers to glow.
The vivid shine of
the silvery crown
Leave rainbows in the dawn!

Adolescence & Adulting - A complex interpretation

Adolescence and adulting is a continuation of life, all twisted and warped around the idea of identity, responsibility and love craving as a human being. Understanding this phase of life is a complex because it's an embodiment of all human emotions. The poems in this section will try to bring out the hidden emotions right from your soul coinciding it with your life. Because they are not just imaginations but experiences of each one of us mended in poetries. Words have also tried to put light on social issues which need to be dealt at an earliest and solved efficiently.

Let's discover the complex interpretation!

12. Love with a Writer

Ever if you adore a writer in life,
Your first light will be mellifluous.
The evening will be unusual,
Resonating in the
writer's rhymes,
The trees will blanket you
with more shade and
The sunbeam will caress your
skin perennially.
The breeze will waltz your
billowed hair,
Even your eyes will convey

the Universe to him.
The writer won't promise
for a pristine journey,
Because he can be
insane sometimes,
With your lovely tales or
with his pen.
He will never say how madly
he loves you, back until,
Your absence made his eyes wet,
And the countless "I love you"
you wrote him
Will not be enough then.
You don't need to decorate
The fragrance filled candles,
Just gift wrap what a writer
yearns the most-
A blank diary and
some murky hues.
If you sincerely love a writer,
Hold him like a gleam
in your eyes for,
If a writer falls for you,
You can never breathe your last.

13. Heartstrings

I crafted a secret garden for us,
Adorned it with love,
It took my patience but

It's ready for whence you come.
The doors have a key,
Fashioned from
our woven souls.
Embracing the
garden's fragrance,
Beneath the frosty wind,
We took the chill off
With a cozy hug.
Pink rose turned red in shyness,
The embers once ignited with love
Glow dimly as we laugh.
That gentle touch
made my body reborn
In the most perfect form.
The grass moves
in steady waves,
As calm as harbor waves;
The depth of sky's hue strengthens,
Ketki flowers bloom in abundance,
Passing unto the eternal cycle of love.
In this garden,
our love burgeon
As a splendid flower,
Blossoming in my sunshine
And breathing in your serene.

14. An Ember in the Cold

Beneath the lucid moon and a murky sky,

Icy wind nudges my skin and bones.

Waiting in the old cabinet

Amidst the Parijat woods,

You came alongside,

covering in a woolen cardigan.

Sitting in a wooden bench

In front of a fiery warm place,

You dropped the cardigan,

I adore your hands and

Do not let you go anywhere.
The cold night borrows
heat from your soul,
And I watch the wine glass
melt in your palm.
As your dew-melded hairs
Touched my dry skin,
Fate reminds me
it's not a fantasy,
I see you you're still there,
it's not a dream.
The night descends
lazy as a bear,
Greeting our bare feet
with cold air.
As our breaths rise and fall
Fire wins over the winter's call,
Aroma of burning logs,
Filled the room
in a big swirl and once again
I'm warmed by the love of your eyes.

15. An Evening Love

The evening goes on like
a perpetual river,
Unconfined like the first love
That flows on and on
splashing love all the way.

Something unsaid,

something unheard,

A few secrets

nothing are shared.

Somewhere or the other

a deep desire has awakened,

Blood rushing through the face

Took my eyesight away and

Floral leaf blushing in the tree,

Disclosed our feelings free.

Lost in the silence of this evening,

We are maddened by our passion.

Lost and carefree is

the silly breeze,

But aware of the glimpses

that we share.

As the evening stretches

A tinge of pleasantly aura,

The sky turns crimson,

The wind runs gentle and

Setting sun throws its

rosy hue in the lake.

The swift falling

shadows of night,

The captivating charm

of the ending.

Remind us to return home,

Still we're obstinate

to depart from the tale that lure.

Willing to be lost

in the evening,

We heard our words fumbling,

For the words have left its habitancy

And can rarely return the place.

16. Beyond the Blue

We are taught by our blind stars,
It's not our flaw you see,
This is the preachment

since centuries
That a man doesn't cry.
Finding beauty in
the colourful world,
He appreciate the flowers,
And adorn them without regret.
He speaks with a soft voice and
Equally hums the ballad,
He's not afraid to cry
Nor does he hide his smile.
He admires poetry
written under a sunset,
But a doctor sounds wiser.
Igniting the war of masculinity,
He has wiped his eyes and
Learnt to smile with a lie.
He owes a beard now but
His tender heart is still a child.
He don't cry anymore
But the leftover tears
were still unsoaked.
He waits for a soulful conversation
To break the silence,
But unaware where to start from.
He burst out in throbbing pain,
Tears drip from silence and
his thoughts unlocked.

He thanked his friend,

in the mirror- his old soft tunes,

For fragmenting the silence,

Ending the war that was fueled.

Reading mirrors was

never that uneasy,

Contemplating every

second of reality

Under the night so breezy.

Beyond the blue,

He might choose the pink hues

Behind his strength,

He might follow his weaknesses.

17. Bleed with Pride

With the charm of immortality

Blood ripped out of the delicate lining,

Discharging the treasure of it all.

As the gush of current flows inward,

The nerve endings got numb,

But seems only a usual visitor.

The charm to bleed

hides pain unseen,

That world may

never manifest.

Once the world

swam in the red,

To nourish its origin and

accouche its offspring,

But in a spur of moment

The entire blood is accursed,

As a fluid so dirty and cursed.

Show me waters

holier than menses -

You will keep searching the Universe

And come back with empty hands,

As the world is better

For the blood that

visits irregular.

Shedding lights on menstruation,

Dissolving the collective shame,

Harnessing power of the cycle,

Lets rename the blood something holy,

As Goddesses dream
when they bleed
But not be nameless anymore,
For it's not only
the pride of Womanhood
But identify of mankind.

18. The Lady that Swears to Death

Veiled in the shades of pink,
She belongs to the world of fairies
in the elfin cave.
Her eyes sparkle

in the beauty of innocence and

Her lips paint words

of soulful communication.

Hairs longer than usual

dipped in velvety black,

Weave into buoyant threads like

an ocean of creative conjuring.

She spoke in a tone of auditory caramel,

Resonating with my soul

to fall in love with.

Millions of death whispered

about her merciless love,

But I was all ears to her

and not any.

Promptly her beauty

vanquished in the darkness,

And calmly she lay me in my grave.

> "*This poetry is inspired from the poem LA BELLE DAM SANS MERCI which in French means 'The beautiful lady without mercy'. More or less the poetry resonate with the same concept written by the literature mastero John Keats, one of my greatest inspiration for all times.*"

19. The Dark Downpour!

As the rain enriches
the sweet brown soil,
People perceiving life
know its pain.
In the earthy
smell of petrichor
We relish the
greenery so serenade.
Grey skies singing melody,
Raindrops drumming
against the canopy,
Aroma rising slowly from
the floral bloom
And we luxuriate
in the comfy room.
But never did
the eyes feel
The pain of
those adorable faces,
Living under a no-roof leaking state.
Shivering in the
frosty winds,
Wrapped in the

torn fabrics,
They search for hope,
a small hope
Under the apartments and
down the drains.
But receives nothing
less than despair
Amongst the dark
voids of pain.

20. In the Whirlwind of Climate Change

The temperature is oscillating
She could not breathe,
She's chocked in destruction,
For evolution of a new state.
Forming the green wonders

She made several wander but,
Multifarious barks have dropped
Without a thought or ponder.
The wider aspect of abundant marine
Burying array of colourful corals,
Tries to fetch a few fresh blue,
Amid the toxins and wastes ensue.
The smog adhere to her lungs
Leading to destruction spontaneous;
Despite this, Nature incarnate as resourceful genius.
She bleeds through the chemicals
That slashes her soul,
Crying with lament
as her own people
Demolish her in foul.
Soon a rage, a wrath unfurls,
Settlements eroded to the ground,
Populations are obliged
to rush their compound.
Violently the sea keeps
thrashing its height,
And the cities submerge
in its demonic plight.
Global warming burning the earth's layers,
CFCs touching the ozone layer.
Concern are raised, opinions followed,
Through agreements countless treaties are signed and

Responsibilities for Nature are warmly assigned.
But race of doomed species again arise,
Management of concerns are kept aside,
So pollution prevails persistently,
And Mother Nature wrecks more steadily.
War against Nature is already lost,
Either it's man or wild,
surviving at any cost.
Still in the midst of all ruins,
She repeats the antiquity of her genesis,
Nurturing the spirit of every species.

21. Silent Cry of the Beauty

Out of the spectacular green,
They are born to this garden,

Flamboyant blossom
outspread the land,
Drenching from the
rich black sand.
But hastily the recreant,
Seizes the freedom of the plant to live.
As he wrenches the stalk,
The leaves fall apart,
Her beauty turned pale,
Her blood unseen,
Her scream unheard,
Her flower that escalated
beauty once, died in a sway
And her body imprisoned in a cold hand.
Her evocative aroma nobody felt,
That silently dwelt in the landscape,
as lonely as the sky.
With the plant advancing to die,
The divine agency arrived
as a miracle, the rain.
Colourless pearls showered
from the sky,
Nourishing the plant
which was still alive.
Unconscious was the rain that fall incessantly -
Blessing the plant to reinvigorate
And overcoming the worst efficiently.

22. Falling Down

Minute drops of rain precipitate,

As it scale down

the earth to reach.

Destined for the flight of fancy;

I'm air- dashed, high up in the sky.

The world is pleasing and

is just so free,

From a place

you look down to see.

Gravity takes it hold

as it always will and,

There you spot a great wall

standing upon the Chinese hill.

Amidst the illusionary crowd,

The sight suddenly shift sideways,

And you see the statue of unity.

In excess of being a hypocrite

Empathy of unity is unseen,

There exist only games

to take over the entity.

Beyond the superiority of wars and

Foraging ahead with zero loathing,

Let us step into Humanity.

But wait! Am I still anticipating?

Now, finally as I take off,

I fall down a little unforeseen,

To see that there is no wall,

no statue or no rain, and

Even a slight thought of Humanity

has NO existence.

23. Who'll Protect Durga?

Like the flickering rays of sunshine,

Piercing the darkest spell of demons,
She arrived the world
as an omniscient being.
Bright eyes with tender heart,
Her grace made the
Lords bow down to her.
She is the manifestation of eleven Rudras,
Carrying eight Basus and twelve Adityas;
Holding the Mitra, Varuna, Indra, Agni
And both the Ashwini Kumars,
She's the female divinity of the Universe.
She wake up with
weapons ten in her hands
The power of fearlessness,
the source of strength,
Holding millions of forces
to rule the sphere.
With the finest quality of burnt offerings,
She provides sacrificial
fruit and honey to her devotee.
Killing the buffalo headed Mahisasura,
She elicits the folklore of Mahalaya,
Protecting the Trilok in her arms.
But who will protect Durga?
With time Durga entangled
in scary ropes and
The world chocked her in cruelty

She ran everywhere,

many watched too

But choose their shameful silence.

Many touched her Pride,

played with her extant,

Bruised her heart and

gave wounded marks,

But she seeks the shelter

of passion, love and peace.

Still everyone bow down and pray to Durga,

In the hope to destroy the demonic rage

Protecting the earth with her valor and courage,

But the query- "who will protect Durga?"

Remained unanswered.

Being envious with insecurities,

And masked up with goodness,

The blind eyes cannot see

Durga's essence

In every being of lady.

Let's not forget that

every girl carries Durga within,

If she can love completely,

she can protest fiercely

She can even urge the Durga within

To protect the self embodiment.

Declining years- A closer step towards Nature

Finally with aging the superior significance of Mother Earth is understood. The declining years is reminder that Nature is home, hearth and sustenance for all creation that echoes with the dying soul and brings the most colourful light of eternity. The footage of Nature and its components will spark a sense of comfort or relaxation which the worldly bonds fail to create.

Witness some of the mind soothing poems of this section

24. The Forest's Call

Come walk with me towards
the woodland manifested abode,
And view the spellbinding Nature
that earth has bestowed.
Relishing in the dreamlike
grandeur that encloses me,
I eagerly tuned to the Nature,
composing the forest's majestic opus.
The murmuring of the trees and rippling streams,
Start a journey in my mind and
I wander into a writer's lovely dreams.
When the sunbeam glisten
the forest's leaves aglow,
I take a nap under
the trees sitting below.
Where trees shades me
From incessant heat and harsh rays,
Let's liberate the mind
To view the Mother Nature's ways.
The pearly drops from heaven
nourishes the life dwelling there,
To safeguard the tender offspring from
hurdles too grim to bear.
Take a seat underneath
the radiant flames of an autumnal tree,
Whose flamboyant hues creates

an innate wonder many come to see.
The chromatic leaves slide down
in a rhythmic course,
Like the cinders losing heat
from their flaming source.
Every leaf wretched for a moment as if,
it was there endmost fate
But the Nature nurtures the earth
for renaissance of a new state.
With the advancing of winter,
the forest befits as a secluded place.
Still, beside the frozen sky
sunburst fall at the tree's base,
Promising the dawn of new life
that calmly waits,
For spring's blossom and rain
to unfold nature's gates.
Amble in the spring forest,
I'll breathe in deep
And promptly, the bliss of Earth
awakens her child from sleep.
Oftentimes, let's respond to the forest's call,
To behold the eternal beauty and miracle of it all,
When I spend more time in Nature,
walking among the trees
I may comprehend the message
carried on a breeze.

Blending my emotion with
the forest's spirit at rebirth,
I too shall procure a life
within this Paradise of Earth.

25. When a Robin visits my gallery

When darkness loses its dignity
And light grows stronger
A robin visits my gallery.

Unconscious of my gazing eyes,
He bit a mealworm into halves and
Drank a dewdrop
from the hibernal grass.
As the flickering shaft
of sunlight falls on him,
A pitch black body
And red accompanying the tail,
Glowed in the glint of sunlight.
He glanced with swift eyes,
And starts a tuneful chirrup,
This morning had ever heard.
His melodies are extravagant
That calms the monotonous dawn.
Holding fears in my heart and
with shaky hands,
I offered him a crumb.
Oh! I wasn't surprised,
He unrolled his feathers and
flew away home.
I gazed him as far as my vision could reach,
With little thought,
What luxury he had brought.
For now when darkness wins over light
And the old city is painted black,
The sweet chirrup of the Robin
Flashes upon my inward sight.

My heart with bliss mumbles with the Robin.

26. The Autumnal Majesty

Amidst the artistic touch of
The October's Golden light,
Blue sky and rainless cloud blushes
Fabricating a glorious sight.

Oak, maples and pumpkins
Ripens to the core and
I saw a beauty unsurpassed,
With Birch and Hemlock,
Tuning their unusual sounds more.
Kinetic leaves in the breeze whisper
Soft adieus as they float down,
Decorating the Nature's carpet
Of pink, red, yellow and brown.
Wispy wind, bunch of eve and Cypress scents
Sets the stage for Cricket's event.
It's the final theme of the destiny,
To sing Ode of the Autumnal majesty.

27. November Mirror

The day ends with the
scent of mud and rain,
Leaving droplets of mist behind
Of damping soil,
chilling breeze and dry hearts.
Under the fading warmth,
winter escalate
Creating a fascinating surrealism in mind.
As the mirror fog swiftly melts,

It transparences the vision.
Now plainly I see my aging body
shivering in the wind,
Yet adoring the wintry tale.
Later the mirror portrays
some harsh truths-
The tormenting soul of the green tress,
Bearing Nature's evil necessity and pain.
Naked trunk standstill with grace,
Well cognizant of the season of bloom.
Looking the fog filled mirror
a second time
I sighed, to let go
the agonies of nature,
For nature will burgeon its greenery,
With the renaissance of a new dawn- the spring.
But my heart aches with a query,
Will the mirror ever show
the dawn of my aging body?

28. Nyctophilia

Gazing at the night sky
with a majestic sight,
I fall for the cavernous
hues of blue every time.
In the realm of tranquility
sunlight halts gaiety,
Reflecting the end of another day.

In the serenade of the black,

the stars are sugars

Scattered gloriously over

the black angel's wings and,

The allure moon glimmering

in her dappled beauty

Spun in a perfect synchrony.

Leisurely the night pours

dreams so immense,

That my mind wanders limitless.

In the aura of artificial light,

I embrace the quietude of night.

The generous velvet of black

embellished the moon and

Seclusion in darkness is

where my heart is safe, my soul serene.

Escaping from the light

that projects fear,

The moon in eternal stoic is my salvation.

With the sightless eyes

the world can never manifest,

What it feels like to experience

the darkness all alone.

They say dark is evil,

that whisper thousands of cries

But the beauty of night is perfect

in a Nyctophile's sky,

29. Spiders and moths

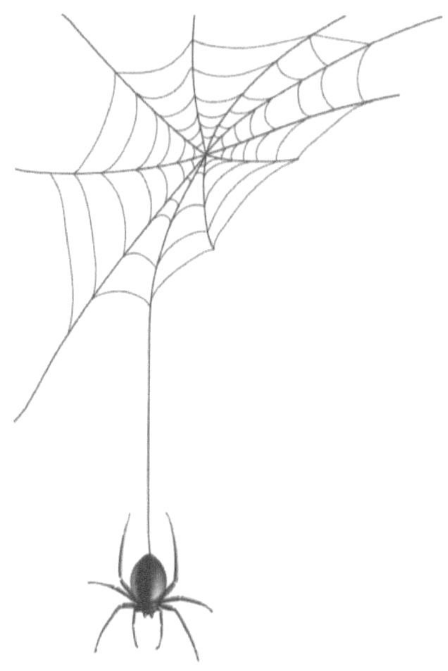

Flimsy threads of cobwebs
tickled around my neck
Pulling and occluding,
the moonlight stained
The spider's web.
Flutter-Flitter, the moth
taste her death,

Despair in the venom underneath,
Torn out wings, broken scales
How dreadful it was!
To see the forewing flapping again.
The spider's web is still stained,
Not in guilt but in
delusions of survival.
The dusk splits the moonlight
From black to blue and
Yet again embraces the dawn.
The sun burned down all the cobwebs,
the threads and the legs,
All that left was the
silent tuning of life,
with a stinging smell of cadaver.

30. The Photograph

Not long ago, I visited my old house,
The silver framed photograph
hangs halt in the wall.
With the wall losing its charm,
The needle gets a wrapping of rust,
Hue with the perfection
of blue fades gradually,
And the slightest edge of the brick
unfolds senescence briskly.

A quick splash of rain cleanses
the grime of the glass,
Visualizing greenery to which,
The dripping water accompanied.
Sparkling water stream,
Flowing amidst the lotus and
a misty ambience
All got captured in the frame.
The sweaters painted
in red and white,
The fogginess around,
apprises the chill of winter,
But the two companions
conceal their love in a smile.
Years had passed as prompt as greased lightning,
And one of them was bound for the stars.
But with few traces left,
The photograph itself is a pleasing reminiscence.

31. Dwelling in the Dark

The night pours blackness unto the life,

Evincing a million thoughts.

We have trusted

the darkest hours,

For a lifetime's bliss calmly appears.

Singing melody in

delightful shocks,

I don't cry in darkness anymore,

I give it the name of blest

In my sombre senility.

For the sake of true courage,

I traversed the bravest part of my soul.

Now the eyes see

beauty in the blackness,

To know how it embraces

The shimmering stars in sky,

All those who moved

closer to the darkness

I can't recall their existence,

As I'm swayed by the

Charisma of sweet darkness,

Far away from the agonizing souls.

32. An Appeal to Death

Oh, Death where is your kiss?

How many more moons will crown in red?

Hearing my whisper,

Will you visit me now?

Beneath the raging despair,

Yearning for your

spectral emergent,

To taste your stale breath

cross my lips.

I ask you, yet once more

Will you cease cruelly ignoring my last wish?

Of your wicked reverie and

irrevocable return,

Dear, Death cover me

into your florets

Motivate my wavering hand to waver more

And carve my endless trail.

Take what belongs to you

What I was unable to pursue.

Of what the Almighty always denied.

Mysterious - Some Hidden Surprises

"*A mystery is a whodunit. You know what happened, but not how or who's behind it. A thriller, or a suspense, is a howdunit. You know what happened, and you usually know who did it, but you keep reading because you want to know how they pulled it off.*"

-M.J. Rose

This section is an additional surprise for my readers to discover mystery, thrill, spooky and suspenseful poetries in the vicinity of life. Everybody has secrets in their life, so why not unfold those dark secrets with these poems?

33. On Highway 13

Intoxicated man in a Bentley
They say had run the light,
That begun
the city cars pileup,

On highway 13 that night.
When broken bodies
shed blood everywhere,
Death arrives in the air.
In the brindled light
of dusk,
when the blues and blacks
become an artwork,
The serenade of winter's song
Screamed out spooky eulogies.

34. Je Veux La Justice

Voidness of the room
Will never make a sound,
but if you hear in serenity
There dwells stories of

Romance and love still abound,

Shattered promises along with

secrets of murders and

shadows still reside.

The beautiful garden is left to decay,

Elongated cobwebs

design the curtains,

Amidst the windows

that is dark and gelid.

Someone still walk in

the crumbling staircase,

The portrait still hangs in the wall

Where the voice of death speaks aloud,

"Je veux la justice"

For the scream that's unheard

And for the crime that's unconfessed.

> *"The title of the poem JE VEUX LA JUSTICE is actually written in French dialect to give an essence of ornamentation. The title actually means 'I want justice', as the voice of the dead people scream for justice for the murder that's unconfessed."*

35. Scream of the Shadow

There is no desire of sleep in my eyes,
Until the victim is resigned,
A dark shadow holding
the silence of crime,
Seek the bones that he must find,
as death shall have no dominion.
Grave lying in the damping soil
Scream under the blood-soaked moon,
Their bones are picked clean and
the clean bones are gone.
Eyes perceive reality,
silent souls weep
And dead men from the coffin creep.
Agitation rips the reality
of the rotten soul,
A disheveled wretch torments and
bleeds with guilt.
The night-lamp casts
a halo of pale light,
With nightmare of murder
glowing in the sight.
The extension of demons must be
dishonored in shame,
Piercing the deceptive veil of fame.
But wait! What did I just hear now?

Is it the darkened shadow shedding tears,

uttering my name!

Yes it do....

Intense fear hammered in the chest,

Droplets of sweat

collapsed my breath and

Menacing aura hold me

in a tightening grip.

But the shadow changes

to bone within a flip

Blind in the vision of death,

moved in a ghastly spell

His story was unnamed,

not the same as mine.

So I wandered lonely in the starry

night finding answers,

What wounds did I, that he is hurt?

Gladioli

Glad to have Gladioli around

My Flowers of Hope

About The Author

Born and raised in the state of lush green tea fields and one horned rhinoceros, that is Assam, Parthiv Rhythm Das is a literature admirer. He is currently pursuing his studies in Agricultural Sciences and ardently writes poetry. Parthiv hosts an Istagram account and owes a blogging media, where he uses his passion for storytelling through his poetry. When he is not writing, Parthiv enjoys listening to music, admiring the Mother Nature, communicating with new people, reading books, dancing, cooking and having some good laughter exercises. Moreover Parthiv is an empowered empath, a feminist and a humanist by nature. He has contributed as a co-author in more than twenty books, wrote several articles and compiled a few books under various publication house.

www.ingramcontent.com/pod-product-compliance
Lightning Source LLC
Chambersburg PA
CBHW021228130726
47988CB00002B/875